it's okay
NOT TO BE OKAY

STUDY GUIDE

Books by Sheila Walsh

It's Okay Not to Be Okay
Praying Women

EIGHT SESSIONS FOR INDIVIDUALS AND GROUPS

it's okay
NOT TO BE OKAY

STUDY GUIDE

Moving Forward One Day at a Time

SHEILA WALSH

BakerBooks
a division of Baker Publishing Group
Grand Rapids, Michigan

Published by Baker Books
a division of Baker Publishing Group
PO Box 6287, Grand Rapids, MI 49516-6287
www.bakerbooks.com

Printed in the United States of America

ISBN: 978-1-5409-0068-5

Study written by Ashley Wiersma
Based on and with material from *It's Okay Not to Be Okay* by Sheila Walsh

20   21   22   23   24   25   26   7   6   5   4   3   2   1

In keeping with biblical principles of creation stewardship, Baker Publishing Group advocates the responsible use of our natural resources. As a member of the Green Press Initiative, our company uses recycled paper when possible. The text paper of this book is composed in part of post-consumer waste.

Contents

From My Heart to Yours

Dear Reader,

If you're like me, there is at least one part of your life that is "not okay" today. Well, let's be honest—there might be many areas that are not okay! Either way, I have written this guide with one central message: *It's okay.* It's okay that life isn't okay. Why? Because there is One who has been okay all along, and that One—Jesus—promises that He is with us, right here.

In the coming sessions, my hope is that you'll be able to let go of the need to convince yourself that you have it all together, that you'll lay down your longing for control over circumstances that (spoiler alert) *can never be controlled*, and that you'll drink deeply of Christ's sufficiency—perhaps for the first time in your life.

The apostle Paul once implored believers at Corinth to follow him as he followed Jesus. That is a life-changing journey we can take together. Let's move toward His goodness, His grace, His enoughness. Let's move together toward the peace only Christ can give. You will never regret a single step taken toward the person of Jesus. The highest possible prayer I can pray for you as you read the pages you hold in your hands is that, by the truth of God's Word and the revelation of the Holy Spirit, you will find that it really is okay not to be okay because Jesus has made you all right with the Father.

If you're ready to journey forward, then let's begin.

With love,
Sheila

I don't know where you're at in life as you read this, but if I could sit down with you for a while, I'd say, "Take a deep breath in and hold it for five seconds, and then let it out. Again. Again."

Then I'd tell you that it *really* is okay not to be okay. That's why Jesus came.

—introduction, *It's Okay Not to Be Okay*

Take the First Step

I held it together until I couldn't anymore. I remember a night in my room in a psychiatric hospital where I literally soaked the floor with my tears. I was bone-tired from pretending to have it all together, from trying to be okay. So, I let God have it. I told Him I was afraid and angry and tired and sad and lonely and confused and everything else I could think of. I didn't edit myself. I just let it all out.

I believe my final words were, "I can't do this anymore."

Rather than feeling rejected by my broken outburst, I felt as if God bent down and said, "I know. I've been waiting."

—chapter 1, *It's Okay Not to Be Okay*

My experience with "pretending to have it all together" left me in a world of trouble—physically, spiritually, emotionally, and relationally. I quite literally came to the end of myself, wondering how on earth I could go on. The journey back to healing and the beginning of wholeness would be long, difficult, and seemingly made up of painfully microscopic steps. But those steps mattered, each one of them, if for no other reason than they kept me from standing still.

So what were the steps? What compelled my feet to take baby steps forward, once I could finally stand up from my bedroom floor? First, this: while I questioned why God would allow my life to career out of control, I still believed He was who He said He was and that He had done what He said He had done. I still believed that Jesus had *actually* come and had *actually* died and had *actually* taken on the weight of my sin.

I still believed that Jesus was sufficient to carry the burden I felt that day.

> **WHAT'S NOT OKAY**
>
> *I'm (still) not enough.*
>
> **WHAT'S BEEN OKAY ALL ALONG**
>
> *Christ is sufficient.*

One to Ponder

When your circumstances confront you and times feel exceedingly tough, do you tend to more readily focus on the things that you *lack* or the things that Jesus *possesses in full*?

How has your posture shifted over time in this regard? What shift do you wish would still occur?

Turning to Scripture

There is perhaps no clearer description of the sufficiency of Jesus than the words the apostle Paul wrote in Colossians 1. Just after reminding the church in Colossae of Jesus's great sacrifice, which redeemed us from the slave market of sin and pain and eternal separation from God, he described in great detail Christ's relationship with God, His relationship with all of creation—including us—and His relationship with the church. Paul wrote:

> The Son is the image of the invisible God, the firstborn over all creation. For in him all things were created: things in heaven and on earth, visible and invisible, whether thrones or powers or rulers or authorities; all things have been created through him and for him.

He is before all things, and in him all things hold together. And he is the head of the body, the church; he is the beginning and the first-born from among the dead, so that in everything he might have the supremacy. For God was pleased to have all his fullness dwell in him, and through him to reconcile to himself all things, whether things on earth or things in heaven, by making peace through his blood, shed on the cross. (vv. 15–20)

Such a magnificent picture of the greatness of Jesus. It might be tempting to read these words and think that Christ wouldn't be able to understand our pain, but that is not true and that is not how Paul lived out his faith. Less than a decade before Paul captured these thoughts, he wrote to the church in Corinth of his misery over the "thorn in the flesh" he had received. It had been causing him so much anguish, but even three heartfelt pleas weren't enough to persuade God to take it away.

We still don't know what that "thorn" was. Was it a physical ailment, such as a chronic pain in his side or the loss of his eyesight, which some theologians speculate was the case? Was it a spiritual battle he couldn't seem to overcome? Was it an emotional or mental health setback that clouded his perspective day by day?

Whatever it was, it bothered him terribly. It would likely bother us terribly too. Continuing to live despite our "thorns" is the issue here.

The first step Paul needed to take was very likely the same step you and I need to take: "Look up! Look to the Lord Jesus. Remember what you believe."

I wonder how many times Paul recounted the truths he believed about Jesus. I wonder if "the hymn of Christ" he wrote in that letter to believers in Colossae flowed with familiarity from his hand.

All things have been created through Him.
All things have been created for Him.
He is before all things.

He holds all things together.

He is the beginning, the middle, the end.

He is sufficient.

He is our redemption.

He is peace with God.

He is Jesus, our Lord.

Oh, that ever-critical first step: whenever we find ourselves struggling and straining to get back to "okay"—when we're afraid and angry, tired and sad, lonely and confused—we can simply remember that Christ has been there all along, and He is sufficient.

Questions for Reflection

Regarding the passage . . .

1. Why do you suppose it mattered to Paul—and thus ought to matter to us—that Christ is "the image of the invisible God"? What encouragement might those words be for you today?

2. Based on the passage printed above, how would you describe what it means that Christ is sufficient?

3. How might Paul's struggles and stresses—painful, debilitating, and heartbreaking though they were—have served to point him toward Christ's sufficiency? What attitudes or assumptions

might keep a person—even the likes of Paul—from seeing things in this way?

_____

_____

Regarding your personal life . . .

It has always comforted me greatly that the likes of the apostle Paul and even Jesus Himself ("He learned obedience from the things which He suffered" [Heb. 5:8 NASB]) strived for a sense of "okay-ness" along the way. Think of Paul, begging God to take away that dreadful thorn in his flesh. Or what about Jesus, who upon facing death on a cross asked God to "take this cup [of suffering] from me" (Luke 22:42)? It seems it is simply part of the human experience to crave steadiness, stability, the sense that things are all right. We want to be okay! We're not okay unless we're okay. And yet we are never promised okay-ness as part of the Christ-following journey; if anything, the opposite is true.

1. What truths do you find in the following verses regarding what "life in Christ" will be like?

   Matthew 10:39

   _____

   _____

   Acts 9:16

   _____

   _____

Romans 8:17

_____

_____

Philippians 1:29

_____

_____

Philippians 3:10

_____

_____

2 Timothy 2:12

_____

_____

1 Peter 2:20

_____

_____

_____

2. In my experience, most believers aren't all that surprised that they are made to suffer in this terribly broken world; what tends to shock them is the manner in which that suffering appears. Can you relate to this idea? What has surprised you about the ways in which you have suffered thus far?

3. Taking into account those bouts of suffering, what has your struggle and straining toward okay-ness looked like? What choices have you made, what attitudes have you assumed, what relationships have you pursued, and what changes have you seen in yourself as you've strived toward feeling all right and okay?

A Petition to Bring to God

Later in the book of Colossians, the apostle Paul issues a beautiful invitation to believers regarding how to begin baby-stepping their way toward Christ.

> Since, then, you have been raised with Christ, set your hearts on things above, where Christ is, seated at the right hand of God. Set your minds on things above, not on earthly things. For you died, and your life is now hidden with Christ in God. When Christ, who is your life, appears, then you also will appear with him in glory.
>
> Put to death, therefore, whatever belongs to your earthly nature: sexual immorality, impurity, lust, evil desires and greed, which is idolatry. Because of these, the wrath of God is coming. You used to walk in these ways, in the life you once lived. But now you must also rid yourselves of all such things as these: anger, rage, malice, slander, and filthy language from your lips. Do not lie to each other, since you have taken off your old self with its practices and have put on the new self, which is being renewed in knowledge in the image of its Creator. (3:1–10)

Close your time in this session with prayer by completing the prompts that follow—either by writing out your thoughts or by speaking your responses aloud. Just as I did, when I found myself desperate and weeping on my hospital floor, give everything to God, earnestly, honestly resolved to hold nothing back.

Father, I long to set my heart on things above, and yet I realize that in order to do so, I first must turn my focus from the "things below." Those things below, those things that have captured my attention and served only to drag me down, include . . .

I also long to put to death all that belongs to my earthly nature, the cravings and desires and apprehensions and fears that clearly are not from You. I confess to You now that more times than not, rather than craving intimacy with Jesus, I crave . . .

Rather than desiring the comfort and growth only You can provide, I find myself desiring . . .

Rather than claiming the boldness that You provide, I have been caving to these same old fears:

I am reminded in this passage from Paul that I am to put off anger, but that's hard! I am still so angry about . . .

I am still so worried about . . .

I am still so confused as to why . . .

And yet, as this passage reminds me, I have put on a whole new self. Just as Christ is the image of You, the invisible God, I am being renewed in the image of You. In light of this truth, Father, please help me to . . .

In the name of the One who is above all else I pray, amen.

Final Thoughts

The baby step—the monumental baby step—I'd like you to take is this: simply consider Christ.

Consider Christ—that's it.
Consider Christ afresh.

If you're in a puddle of tears on your bedroom floor, *consider Christ afresh.*

If you're tending to a chronically ill child, *consider Christ afresh.*

If you're struggling financially, *consider Christ afresh.*

If you're battling the monster of an addiction, *consider Christ afresh.*

If you're full of rage and feeling out of control, *consider Christ afresh.*

If you're staring at that half gallon of ice cream, thinking you might just down the whole thing, *consider Christ afresh.* (And pick a smaller spoon!)

If you're stretched so thin you're sure you've all but disappeared, *consider Christ afresh.*

If you're falling prey to the comparison game again this week, *consider Christ afresh.*

Consider Christ, who is sufficient.

Christ, who is *arkeo.*[1]

Christ, who is enough.

In response to Paul's third request for that devastating thorn to be removed, God said, "My grace is sufficient for you" (2 Cor. 12:9).

God's grace.

God's love.

God's perspective.

God's Son.

God's *sufficiency* is all that we need.

As we weaken, His strength comes rushing in. May we find our true strength in Him.

Making These Themes Your Own

At the end of each session, this section will remind you of the action steps presented along the way. My hope is that reading these things

18

laid out together will serve as a useful resource for you as you pray and think about which items to include in your life.

Please don't allow these end-of-session cues to burden or condemn you; these are not to-do lists, my friend. Instead, allow them to spark in your imagination a handful of ways the content you just covered might serve you well in the days and weeks to come.

> **arkeo** *[ar-'keh-o]*
> Be content, be enough, suffice, be sufficient.

- Confess one or more "earthly nature" habits to your heavenly Father, and allow Him to put them to death.
- Picture yourself stepping into a whole new self, as Galatians 2:20 says we have been given. Walk around in that new self a bit. What is true for that new self that wasn't true for the old?
- Carve out several minutes during your day today to simply consider Christ. What realities does His wholehearted sacrifice on the cross usher in for you? What sense might that sacrifice make of your pain?

two

Admit That You Are Stuck and Struggling

There are so many things that happen in life that feel like the slamming of a door.

> The end of a friendship you cherished.
> The loss of a job.
> A divorce you never saw coming.
> A child cutting you out of their life.
> A devastating health issue.

The circumstances are different for each person, but the feelings of being rejected, isolated, or heartbroken are crushing. What makes many of these situations much harder to bear is that you had no choice, no say in the matter.

—chapter 2, *It's Okay Not to Be Okay*

The reason it is absolutely critical to do what was mentioned in the last session—to consider Christ afresh—is because life has a way of pulling the rug right out from under our feet, leaving us breathless, flat on our back. Speaking from personal experience, sobbing into the carpet, tears streaming down your cheeks, is a lonely place to be. *Surely nobody has ever known this much pain,* you think. *Surely I'm the first to suffer this way! I'll never get out of this mess I'm in. Nobody's coming. Nobody sees me. No one cares.*

And yet, as we'll see in this session on feeling stuck, God *always* sticks right by your side.

> WHAT'S NOT OKAY
> *I'm isolated, alone.*
>
> WHAT'S BEEN OKAY ALL ALONG
> *Christ is here with me.*

One to Ponder

What assumptions or beliefs tend to follow for you once you've perceived that you're alone in your pain?

How many of the items you noted could be considered useful, life-giving thoughts?

Turning to Scripture

Some years ago, I noticed an interesting trend regarding my perceptions of God. When things were going well and I was feeling happy and positive, the prevailing thought was, *God must love me so much!* When things were not going well and I was feeling down, the prevailing thought was, *Where is God? I'm all alone.*

Whenever my circumstances were positive, I exhibited positive emotions. Whenever my circumstances were negative, I exhibited negative emotions. No surprise, this was a confusing way to live. Eventually, I discovered that the reason for this wild swing in perception was a little thing called *focus*, focus on what I was thinking about. At all times and in all situations, I was focused on the circumstances of my life. Not a wise or faith-filled approach.

In the following passage from 2 Corinthians, see if you can spot what the apostle Paul said is *supposed* to be the direct object of our gaze.

But we have this treasure in jars of clay to show that this all-surpassing power is from God and not from us. We are hard pressed on every side, but not crushed; perplexed, but not in despair; persecuted, but not abandoned; struck down, but not destroyed. We always carry around in our body the death of Jesus, so that the life of Jesus may also be revealed in our body. For we who are alive are always being given over to death for Jesus' sake, so that his life may also be revealed in our mortal body. So then, death is at work in us, but life is at work in you.

It is written: "I believed; therefore I have spoken." Since we have that same spirit of faith, we also believe and therefore speak, because we know that the one who raised the Lord Jesus from the dead will also raise us with Jesus and present us with you to himself. All this is for your benefit, *so that the grace that is reaching more and more people may cause thanksgiving to overflow to the glory of God.*

Therefore we do not lose heart. Though outwardly we are wasting away, yet inwardly we are being renewed day by day. For our light and momentary troubles are achieving for us an eternal glory that far outweighs them all. So we fix our eyes not on what is seen, but on what is unseen, since what is seen is temporary, but what is unseen is eternal. (4:7–18)

This sentence gets me every time I read it: "We fix our eyes not on what is seen," Paul says, "but on what is unseen, since what is seen is temporary, but what is unseen is eternal."

I wish I could have those words tattooed on my soul and the inside of my eyelids!

> **skopeo** *[skop-'eh-o]*
> To take aim at, regard. To take heed, look upon, mark.

To fix our eyes is to do more than physically see, more than give something a passing glance. It is to regard a thing as important, to see not with eyes but with faith. It is less about sight than insight,

22

less about what is natural than what is supernatural, even divine. It is to say, "Circumstances be what they may, I'm staring at You, Lord, and refusing to look away. My mind is set, my faith is sure, my gaze is set. I'm looking. I'm focused. I'm here."

Questions for Reflection

Regarding the passage . . .

1. What is the difference between being "hard pressed" but not "crushed," or being "perplexed" but not "in despair," or being "persecuted" but not "abandoned," or being "struck down" but not "destroyed"?

2. In the text above, what does Paul cite as the reason that we are not crushed, left to our despair, abandoned, and destroyed? (I've inserted an asterisk before and after the relevant verse to point the way.)

3. In what way(s) can you relate to the idea of carrying "in our body the death of Jesus," this sense that the pervasive exposure to difficulty and death, to trouble and trials, to chaos and mayhem and pain that Jesus himself endured while on earth, is also our lot to bear?

4. What encouragement might you take from the fact that (1) Jesus understands the troubles you presently face, and (2) these troubles will not win the day?

Regarding your personal life . . .

1. When you have felt alone in your struggles, what have you been focused on? Why does our human nature seem to dictate that we obsess over our circumstances instead of fixing our eyes on the One who holds them all?

2. What do you wish God would do to assure you of His presence? If His suggestion box were open, what suggestion might you make?

3. Blaise Pascal, the great seventeenth-century mathematician, physicist, inventor, and theologian, once wrote regarding our heavenly Father's presence that "God is an infinite sphere, the center of which is everywhere, the circumference nowhere." What do you find in Psalm 139:7–12 to support this assertion by Pascal? Further, what might change in your posture toward

trials if you believed that these sentiments—both from Pascal and from the Word of God—were true?

A Petition to Bring to God

To reinforce this session's central idea, let's center our minds on this thought: there is a reason we are to fix our gaze on Jesus, which is that the longer we fix our gaze on Him and not on our circumstances, the more likely it is that we will draw near to Him instead of drawing near to fear and despair. And an amazing thing happens when we draw near to God, to His Son, to His Spirit. God then draws near to us.

In the book of James, the apostle James tells believers in impassioned pleas to break off their friendship with the world—its ineffective evaluations and "solutions"—and to cling instead to friendship with God. I can almost sense a "compassionate frustration" in his words, something akin to his saying, "Come on, people . . . *please* don't get this wrong!" He wrote:

> What causes quarrels and what causes fights among you? Is it not this, that your passions are at war within you? You desire and do not have, so you murder. You covet and cannot obtain, so you fight and quarrel. You do not have, because you do not ask. You ask and do not receive, because you ask wrongly, to spend it on your passions. You adulterous people! Do you not know that friendship with the world is enmity with God? Therefore whoever wishes to be a friend of the world makes himself an enemy of God. Or do you suppose it is to no purpose that the Scripture says, "He yearns jealously over the spirit that he has made to dwell in us"? But he gives more grace. Therefore it says, "God opposes the proud but gives grace to the humble." Submit yourselves therefore to God. Resist the devil, and

IT'S OKAY NOT TO BE OKAY STUDY GUIDE

he will flee from you. Draw near to God, and he will draw near to you. (4:1–8 ESV)

If James's words were lyrics to a song, they would sound like utter chaos until that last verse. All we would hear is noise, turmoil, judgment, and a verbal beating until those last few phrases appeared. But with the line "submit yourselves therefore to God," all would begin to level out. Sweet harmony. Notes played perfectly. Utter peace. Why? Because God's presence is full of who He is. In God's presence, we find other things.

What do the following verses reveal about the things that always accompany the presence of God? Write down your discoveries in the spaces provided.

Romans 15:13

_____

_____

1 Corinthians 1:25

_____

_____

Ephesians 6:13

_____

_____

1 John 4:8

_____

_____

In your present circumstances, which of these divine resources are you most in need of? Check one or as many as you need to from the options below.

- Hope
- Peace
- Joy
- Power
- Strength
- Wisdom
- Protection
- Love

In James's passage above, we are reminded that we do not have because we do not ask (v. 2). Isn't that a profound idea? We do not have because we do not ask. Why don't we simply turn and ask God?

Keeping in mind the divine resource you crave—wisdom or power or protection or love—bring that request before God. Pray through the prompts that follow, or pray the words that are on your own heart.

Heavenly Father, You are good and You are God, and my posture here before You reflects the humility I feel in Your presence. Thank You for being all-knowing. Thank You for being all-powerful. Thank You for being all-present. Thank You for being here with me now.

I confess to You, Lord, my tendency to . . .

_____

_____

I confess to You these things that distract me from fixing my eyes on You:

_____

_____

I thank You that whenever I am _____ *, You are*

_____ *.*

I come to You now as a child in need of . . .

_____

_____

Would You please provide me with . . .

_____

_____

Thank You for being a God who keeps His promises. Thank You for drawing near to me as I draw near to You. Change me, Lord. Transform me. As I fix my eyes on You, may I be renewed, renewed, renewed. Amen.

Final Thoughts

Perhaps you can relate to a certain set of behaviors that some people cycle through once a bad thing comes their way. They suffer. They despair. They complain to whoever happens to be nearby. Then they suffer some more. Then they despair some more. Then they complain some more.

I understand. I've been there too, but I know now that we are offered a better way.

If you're open to an experiment, for this week, embrace a different way of being. Enter God's presence expectantly, trusting that there you will find all you need.

Making These Themes Your Own

- Even from the pit of despair, practice fixing your gaze on Jesus. What do you see as you take Him in?
- Ask God for the divine resources you need to keep your gaze trained on Him.
- Seize every opportunity that God provides for practicing these resources. If He provides opportunity to practice hope, seize it. If joy, seize it. If wisdom, seize it.

three

Change the Way You Think

We pursue renewal through the transforming of our minds. You might be tempted to ask, "What's wrong with my mind?" You're smart, well educated, and computer savvy, with endless information at your fingertips. . . . The problem is not a lack of information; it's a lack of renewal.

—chapter 3, *It's Okay Not to Be Okay*

In the world of psychology, one of the most important models is known as CBT, or cognitive behavioral therapy. At its core, this model simply says that it's not what we *feel* about an event or how we *behave* in light of an event that matters most but rather what we *think* about the event that has occurred. Take this example from everyday life. It is 2:00 a.m. You are lying in bed, asleep and alone, when you are wakened by a very loud sound. Clearly, something has crashed to the floor unexpectedly, but you're not entirely sure what it is.

Do you assume that the crash was due to:

- a burglar entering your home and tripping over something in the dark on his way to assault you?
- your aging dog who struggles to see clearly trying to get at his food supply again, getting tangled up in the lamp cord, and causing it to tumble to the ground?

> **WHAT'S NOT OKAY**
>
> *I am powerless to overcome my struggles.*
>
> **WHAT'S BEEN OKAY ALL ALONG**
>
> *God promises transformation, unfolding in me day by day.*

Certainly, your life experience to date will factor into your thinking, but in general, which option would you choose?

The CBT model would analyze you thus:

- If you think that the loud crash was caused by an intruder, then you will feel afraid and will adjust your behaviors accordingly, either by lying there frozen, paralyzed by fear, or by preparing yourself for an outright battle with this intruder who means you harm. You will then suffer a terribly restless night, as you fail to fall back asleep.
- If you think that the loud crash was caused by your sensory-impaired four-legged friend, then you will feel a fleeting sense of frustration as you think, *Looks like I'll have a mess to clean up in the morning.* After making sure the aforementioned dog is okay, you will ease back into a good night's sleep, a touch annoyed but generally amused.

Our *thoughts* govern our *feelings*, which then govern the *actions* we choose to take. Those *actions* then bring about *consequences*, which will either *bless* or *burden* our lives. Pretty hefty load those little thoughts carry, don't you think? What we think *in fact* is what we become. As I said, this model is attributed to the world of psychology. But as we'll see shortly, its true inventor was God.

31

In this session, we will explore the power of our thoughts in relationship to the events we experience. What does "taking our thoughts captive" mean to us practically? What thoughts should we be thinking instead? What do we do with thoughts that refuse to be wrangled? Do we really have control over such things?

One to Ponder

Like an advertising jingle you just can't get out of your head, what thought seems to be on repeat in your mind?

If you were able to permanently replace that thought with another thought, what would that replacement thought be?

Turning to Scripture

In his letter to believers in Rome, an epistle considered by most Bible scholars to be the most influential and important book of the New Testament, the apostle Paul lays out in painstaking detail the universal need for the good news of Christ, the benefit to society of Christ-followership, the purpose of the law in the new covenant, and how the gospel relates to God's chosen nation, Israel. And then he comes to the "so what." So what do all of these weighty ideas mean for the individual believer longing to please God?

According to Paul, they mean many things. They mean service through spiritual gifts. They mean contributing meaningfully and lovingly to society. They mean holding out hope for a beautiful future. They mean carrying the message of grace to the world. But *before* all these things is one *primary* thing, and that thing has to do with our minds.

Paul wrote:

I appeal to you therefore, brothers, by the mercies of God, to present your bodies as a living sacrifice, holy and acceptable to God, which is your spiritual worship. Do not be conformed to this world, but be transformed by the renewal of your mind, that by testing you may discern what is the will of God, what is good and acceptable and perfect. (Rom. 12:1–2 ESV)

No longer are we to approach God with bleeding animals sacrificed in His name. For those of us who are "in Christ," participants in the covenant of grace, the expected sacrifice is our *bodies*—it is our flesh, our souls, our minds. "Love so amazing, so divine," wrote seventeenth-century British minister and hymn writer Isaac Watts, "demands my soul, my life, my all."[1]

Every cell.

Every breath.

Every thought.

All of our all—that's what we offer Christ.

Questions for Reflection

Regarding the passage . . .

1. What do you think is meant by a full-bodied sacrifice that is "holy and acceptable to God"? What type of sacrifice might God accept?

2. What is Paul implying about the world's ways when he cautions believers not to be "conformed to this world"?

3. Paul forms a connection here between minding our thought life and coming to understand the will of God. Through what other means have you seen someone—perhaps even yourself—try to know the will of God?

_____

_____

_____

Regarding your personal life . . .

1. What words come to mind when you think of the term *renewal*?

_____

_____

_____

2. What is the prevailing emotion you experience as you meditate on the idea of a personal, spiritual, inner-world renewal of your mind?
   - Enthusiasm: "This is *exactly* what I need."
   - Hopefulness: "If anyone can change me, it is God."
   - Curiosity: "I wonder what, specifically, will change."
   - Skepticism: "I've tried everything else. Maybe *this* will work."
   - Cynicism: "Quick fixes never stick, and I suspect that's what this is."

3. The word here for renewal is *anakainosis*, pronounced an-ak-'ah-ee-no-sis. It's a mouthful, but at its core is this simple concept: renovation. Renovation! Who doesn't like a renovation!

What do the following verses say regarding who bears the responsibility
for renewing our minds? Circle the relevant words/phrases that stand out to
you.

> **anakainosis**
> *[an-ak-'ah-ee-no-sis]* To
> renovate, renew, restore.

> Create in me a pure heart, O God,
>   and renew a steadfast spirit within me.
> Do not cast me from your presence
>   or take your Holy Spirit from me.
> Restore to me the joy of your salvation
>   and grant me a willing spirit, to sustain me. (Ps. 51:10–12)

But when the kindness and love of God our Savior appeared, he saved
us, not because of righteous things we had done, but because of his
mercy. He saved us through the washing of rebirth and renewal by
the Holy Spirit, whom he poured out on us generously through Jesus
Christ our Savior, so that, having been justified by his grace, we might
become heirs having the hope of eternal life. (Titus 3:4–7)

That, however, is not the way of life you learned when you heard
about Christ and were taught in him in accordance with the truth
that is in Jesus. You were taught, with regard to your former way of
life, to put off your old self, which is being corrupted by its deceitful
desires; to be made new in the attitude of your minds; and to put on
the new self, created to be like God in true righteousness and holi-
ness. (Eph. 4:20–24)

4. Which of your current thought-life practices *cooperate* with
   the Spirit's work in renewing your mind and which *contradict*
   it? Take a look at the examples that have been provided for you
   on the next page, and then log your insights on the rows that
   follow.

Thought Pattern	Cooperation	Contradiction
Example: "I'll never get out of this emotional pit I'm in."		Whether I intended to or not, somewhere along the way I signed up for death, even as the Spirit is all about life.
Example: "I don't know how I'll ever recover from the pain of this divorce, but I believe that you know, God."	God says that He is my protection and my comfort, my refuge and my safe place. I'm choosing to believe that is so.	

5. What encouragement can you take from the fact that this mind-renewal process you're exhorted to engage in does not rest on *your* shoulders, reside on *your* to-do list, or sit at *your* feet? (Anyone other than me shouting, "Thank you Jesus!"?)

A Petition to Bring to God

There is such promise here. I pray you sense it; I do. Our thoughts, which, as we've seen, govern everything else that happens to us, can be renewed. We can learn to think differently! Which means we can then learn to feel differently too. When we feel differently, then we behave differently, and when our behavior shifts, we're made brand-new. What's more, as we've discovered, the responsibility is not on us to accomplish this astounding work.

If you've never trusted God, by His Spirit, to renovate your thoughts, then may I invite you into the practice today? Here and now, just you and God?

What follows are several aspects of life that commonly present struggles for us. What thoughts come to mind as you consider each category? What "truths" do you tell yourself? Some thoughts will be useful, some will be useless, some will fall somewhere in between. Your job, after logging the thoughts that you think related to the categories that apply to you, is to ask the Lord what action to take.

Should you keep the thought?

Should you toss it?

Should you add the thought to how you normally think?

Spend a few moments in prayer, asking God for divine insight, and then place the appropriate letter beside each thought: *K*, to keep the thought; *T*, to toss the thought; or *A*, to add this new thought to the mix.

Thoughts I find myself thinking regarding my . . .

Vocation

_____

_____

_____

Marriage

_____

_____

_____

Parenting

_____

_____

_____

Friendships

_____

_____

_____

Devotion to Christ

_____

_____

_____

Future

_____

_____

_____

Past

_____

_____

_____

Skills, Talents, and Giftings

_____

_____

_____

Potential

_____

_____

_____

Family of Origin

_____

_____

_____

_____

Struggles

_____

_____

_____

Worthiness/Value

_____

_____

_____

Ability to Change

_____

_____

_____

Now, remember to label your thoughts:

K: keep the thought
T: toss the thought
A: add this new thought to the mix

Final Thoughts

In my book *It's Okay Not to Be Okay*, I endeavored to explain this odd balance I'm trying to strike between reminding us that it really is okay not to be okay and encouraging us to allow the transforming work of God's Spirit to have full access to every part of our lives. Here is what I wrote: "You may be tempted to ask, 'Why did you call this book *It's Okay Not to Be Okay* if now you're telling me I have to change?' Good question! The answer is simple. It's not an issue of judgment, it's a matter of freedom. Christ wants you to be free. Free from condemning thoughts, free from compulsive behaviors, free to be who you really are, free to live your crazy, beautiful life."[2]

Go back and look at the thoughts you intend to keep and also the thoughts you were prompted to add. Do you see the theme of freedom peeking through? Useful thoughts are freeing thoughts, and it is for freedom that we've been set free.

In Galatians 5:1, the apostle Paul wrote, "So Christ has truly set us free. Now make sure that you stay free, and don't get tied up again in slavery to the law" (NLT). That little phrase "stay free" helps me, and I'd venture a guess it can help you too. In the days to come, as you detect yourself following the downward spiral of negative thoughts, pause just long enough to whisper that reminder: "Stay free."

Stay free, beloved one. You're no longer a slave.
Stay free, cherished one. Your freedom was bought with a price.
Stay free, holy one. The Spirit can capture your thoughts.
Stay free, righteous one. Let God's work have its full way.

Making These Themes Your Own

- Remember the truth that our minds can be renewed. Speak it aloud if you must: "My mind can be renewed. My mind can be renewed. My mind can be renewed."
- By the power of His Spirit, ask God to remove the lies from your thinking and to replace each one with His truth.

four

Face the What-Ifs
Even If You Are Afraid

I wonder what the what-ifs are in your life. Fear and the questions that give it fuel hold us back from stepping out in faith and living the life we long for. I think we're afraid we'll get it wrong, be misunderstood or rejected, or fail. The reality is, all of those things are possible, but they don't have to stop us.

—chapter 4, *It's Okay Not to Be Okay*

Whenever I talk with people about this need to "stay free," to allow the Holy Spirit to utterly transform our way of thinking, to participate in an all-out renovation of the mind, the response I hear more than any other is this: "But what if . . . ?"

But what if he leaves?
But what if I fail?
But what if they win?
But what if I lose my job?

But what if my kid never comes home?

But what if I wind up alone?

"I'd give God free rein in my thought life," the pushback goes, "but what if I do and then wind up worse off than I was before?"

We want to believe that God really is working all things to our good, that He indeed is bringing us to a place of spiritual completion and perfection, that He hasn't lost our number, that He isn't unaware of our suffering, that He'll come through for us in the end. Really, we do.

> **WHAT'S NOT OKAY**
>
> *I'm buried in "What-ifs."*
>
> **WHAT'S BEEN OKAY ALL ALONG**
>
> *The Spirit that resides in us is not of fear but of power and love and self-control.*

Simultaneously, we want something else. We want to have a backup plan in place, just in case.

And so we come up with a litany of hypotheticals, a laundry list of what-ifs that we care for like a helpless pet. We protect them and watch over them. We nurture those what-ifs as though our lives depended on our ability to keep them fueled, to keep them close, to keep them afloat.

What we can't possibly realize in the moment is that each time we focus on our beloved what-ifs, we remove our dependence from God.

One to Ponder

What has been your go-to what-if throughout the years? How have you guarded it?

Turning to Scripture

If you've followed Jesus for any significant length of time, then you likely have come across 2 Timothy 1:7, which says this: "For God gave us a spirit not of fear but of power and love and self-control" (ESV). The New International Version reads, "For the Spirit God gave us does not make us timid, but gives us power, love and self-discipline." Either way, we tend to interpret that verse solely on what we receive. We don't have a spirit of fear. We don't have to be afraid. We've been given a spirit of power. We've been given a spirit of love. We've been given a spirit of glorious self-control. (Some translations call that last bit "a sound mind.")

And while these claims are indeed true—it is true that the Spirit living inside of us isn't a friend of fear—there is more to the story here. The verse's context says this:

> Paul, an apostle of Christ Jesus by the will of God, in keeping with the promise of life that is in Christ Jesus,
>
> To Timothy, my dear son:
>
> Grace, mercy and peace from God the Father and Christ Jesus our Lord.
>
> I thank God, whom I serve, as my ancestors did, with a clear conscience, as night and day I constantly remember you in my prayers. Recalling your tears, I long to see you, so that I may be filled with joy. I am reminded of your sincere faith, which first lived in your grandmother Lois and in your mother Eunice and, I am persuaded, now lives in you also.
>
> For this reason I remind you to fan into flame the gift of God, which is in you through the laying on of my hands. For the Spirit God gave us does not make us timid, but gives us power, love and self-discipline. So do not be ashamed of the testimony about our Lord or of me his prisoner. Rather, join with me in suffering for the gospel, by the power of God. (vv. 1–8)

The exhortation Paul is giving to Timothy—and to us—is broader than a simple reminder not to be afraid. Let's dive in.

Questions for Reflection

Regarding the passage . . .

44

1. Revisit the opening lines of Paul's letter to Timothy. How would you sum up his posture as he begins his correspondence?

   _____

   _____

2. Eventually, Paul arrives at the thrust of his point by saying, "For this reason . . ." What reason, exactly, is Paul referring to?

   _____

   _____

3. Following verse 7, regarding the Spirit that resides in us not being one of fear but of power and love and self-control, Paul makes two quite interesting statements. Write them here.

   _____

   _____

4. Given this broader context, what is Paul saying that the *purpose* of this lack of fear and the presence of power and love and self-control is?

   _____

   _____

What an amazing revelation it has been for me that the fearlessness I know in Jesus is for a far greater good than my private peace of mind. A spirit of fearlessness has been given to us so that we can join Jesus in His suffering—in His *sugkakopatheo*, in the Greek—so

sugkakopatheo
[soong-kak-op-ath-'eh-o]
A hardship in company with.

that we can be bold in sharing the Good News of His rescue and in using our gifts.

Regarding your personal life . . .

1. What spiritual calling, insights, or gifts tend to get suppressed in your life when you are operating from a place of fear, a place of anxiety, a place of what-if?

_____

_____

2. How have you seen things like power and love and self-control overcome the sway of fear in your life? Take a few moments to capture a memory before moving on.

_____

_____

3. Why would God want us to operate from a posture of divine power and love at all times, never once caving to anxiety and fear?

_____

_____

4. What does the passage below imply about the fact that it is possible to live in this seemingly impossible state of never being afraid?

Come to me, all you who are weary and burdened, and I will give you rest. Take my yoke upon you and learn from me, for I am gentle and humble in heart, and you will find rest for your souls. For my yoke is easy and my burden is light. (Matt. 11:28–30)

A Petition to Bring to God

If you're like me, then all this talk of living without fear sounds wonderful, even as you honestly cannot fathom that such a reality is possible for you. Enter baby steps. Remember, I gave my book *It's Okay Not to Be Okay* the subtitle *Moving Forward One Day at a Time*. No giant leaps forward, my friend. No, we are moving *slowly*, you and I. Slowly but surely.

Here is this session's baby step: if you want to hold on to your what-if habit (no judgment from this end), then might you at least swap out the nature of your what-ifs for a while? My challenge—my *invitation*—to you is this: tell God your most pressing what-if these days and then sit, quietly and expectantly, until He offers you a different, more hope-filled what-if.

You might say, "God, my biggest what-if today is 'What if I try and fail?'"

Okay, so there it is. You are afraid to try and fail in an endeavor you're compelled to explore. Tell God the whole sordid truth. And then . . . wait.

This is the hardest part.

Waiting.

Still waiting.

Hang in there; you're doing great.

Child . . .

Did you hear that? It's the still, small voice of God!

What if you try in My power and succeed?

What an invitation.

My point is this: for once, give the Matthew 11:28–30 promise a try. Go to God with your burdensome what-ifs and see if He doesn't supernaturally lighten your load. I've given room below for capturing your thoughts, but if you're already clear on the what-ifs you want to lay down, then don't bother writing; just pray.

My current what-if:

_____

_____

_____

The what-if God offered instead:

_____

_____

_____

My current what-if:

_____

_____

_____

The what-if God offered instead:

_____

_____

_____

My current what-if:

_____

_____

_____

The what-if God offered instead:

_____

_____

_____

My current what-if:

_____

_____

_____

The what-if God offered instead:

_____

_____

_____

My current what-if:

_____

_____

_____

The what-if God offered instead:

_____

_____

_____

Final Thoughts

May I offer a parting caution, one I've picked up by personal experience? As you begin with this grand what-if swap with God, inevitably the time will come when you are just *sure* that one of your old, beloved, drag-you-down what-ifs is actually coming true. Your greatest fear is unfolding, you're certain, right before your eyes. My caution is this: refuse to pick up that old what-if again. Leave it at the feet of God.

Even if it doesn't seem to be the case, God is moving. He is orchestrating. He is at work. He sees you. He sees *it*—the unfolding you've dreaded most. And He cares.

Trust that care. Trust it to envelop you in just the right way, at just the right time, with God, as always, in control.

Making These Themes Your Own

- Speak aloud your worst what-if, but do so as a prayer to your loving Father.
- Invite God to swap out your fear-based what-if for one that is full of faith.

SESSION

five

Let Go of What You Can't Control

I believe the mercy of God allows us at some point in life to hit the wall and, when everything else falls apart, we are held by His mercy. Sometimes we reach that place at the bottom of a bottle or in the wrong person's arms. Sometimes we reach it when we realize that we are resentful of the people who don't notice how much we're doing for them and for God. I reached it on the floor of my room in a psych hospital. However we get there, it's devastating. Everything that has made sense until that point in life is now exposed as a sham. For me, that agonizing, lonely place where I, like Elijah, asked God to take my life became the place where I heard that still, small voice, that whisper: *I love you. Always have. Always will. Rest for a while. Let go.*

—chapter 5, *It's Okay Not to Be Okay*

I probably don't have to tell you that the reason the great what-if exchange I mentioned in the last session was difficult for me is that handing over my beloved what-ifs for a set of what-ifs based on things such as faith and hope and life felt like a colossal loss of control. It felt this way because it *was* this way—or at least that's how it seemed to me.

You can imagine my devastation over coming to the realization that my illusions of control were just that . . . illusions. I'd never been in control to begin with!

Thankfully, what I learned was that handing over my what-ifs was the scariest part of the great what-if exchange. Trusting the God who had always been in control to simply stay in control? By contrast, that was a breeze.

One to Ponder

What is the difference between the self-control that is praised in Scripture and the type of obsessive, clingy, circumstance-wrangling control that God asks us to relinquish to Him?

Which of these two types of control comes more naturally to you and why?

Turning to Scripture

In the book of Hebrews, we find beautiful and necessary reminders of what we have when all we have is Christ. Christ is greater than the prophets, the writer tells us. He is greater than the angels. He is greater than Moses. He is greater than the law. The control over our circumstances we long for? It's much better left with Him.

Hebrews 10 says:

Therefore, brothers and sisters, since we have confidence to enter the Most Holy Place by the blood of Jesus, by a new and living way opened for us through the curtain, that is, his body, and since we have a great priest over the house of God, let us draw near to God with a sincere heart and with the full assurance that faith brings, having our hearts sprinkled to cleanse us from a guilty conscience and having our bodies washed with pure water. Let us hold unswervingly to the hope we profess, for he who promised is faithful. And let us consider how we may spur one another on toward love and good deeds, not giving up meeting together, as some are in the habit of doing, but encouraging one another—and all the more as you see the Day approaching.

If we deliberately keep on sinning after we have received the knowledge of the truth, no sacrifice for sins is left, but only a fearful expectation of judgment and of raging fire that will consume the enemies of God. Anyone who rejected the law of Moses died without mercy on the testimony of two or three witnesses. How much more severely do you think someone deserves to be punished who has trampled the Son of God underfoot, who has treated as an unholy thing the blood of the covenant that sanctified them, and who has insulted the Spirit of grace? For we know him who said, "It is mine to avenge; I will repay," and again, "The Lord will judge his people." It is a dreadful thing to fall into the hands of the living God.

Remember those earlier days after you had received the light, when you endured in a great conflict full of suffering. Sometimes you were publicly exposed to insult and persecution; at other times you stood side by side with those who were so treated. You suffered along with those in prison and joyfully accepted the confiscation of your property, because you knew that you yourselves had better and lasting possessions. So do not throw away your confidence; it will be richly rewarded.

You need to persevere so that when you have done the will of God, you will receive what he has promised. For,

> "In just a little while,
>   he who is coming will come
>   and will not delay."

And,

> "But my righteous one will live by faith.
>   And I take no pleasure
>   in the one who shrinks back."

But we do not belong to those who shrink back and are destroyed, but to those who have faith and are saved. (vv. 19–39)

Questions for Reflection

Regarding the passage . . .

1. In the first part of the passage, what are the three "let us" statements made by the writer of Hebrews?

   • Let us:

   _____

   _____

   • Let us:

   _____

   _____

   • Let us:

   _____

   _____

2. What do you suppose would happen to a person's control issues if he or she were faithful to uphold these three "let us" commands?

   _____

   _____

3. Later in the passage, we find phrases that speak to God's vengeance. What do these words tell us about who is actually in control of the world? What types of situations are noted as being within God's realm of control?

_____

_____

_____

4. What reward(s) does the writer of Hebrews allude to for those who persevere in Christ?

_____

_____

_____

Regarding your personal life . . .

1. The writer of Hebrews encourages believers not to "throw away your confidence" but instead to persevere. The word here for confidence is *parrhesia*, which means outspokenness, bluntness, the tendency to speak freely about one's faith in Jesus. Based on personal experience, what might throwing away confidence look like?

> **parrhesia** *[par-rhay-'see-ah]*
> Outspokenness, frankness, bluntness, assurance, confidence.

What might compel a person to throw away confidence in Christ?

_____

_____

_____

2. Given the circumstances you presently find yourself in, how close are you today to throwing your confidence away?

3. The writer concludes his thoughts with the reminder that "we do not belong to those who shrink back and are destroyed, but to those who have faith and are saved" (v. 39). What is the primary emotion you experience as you take in this reminder? Encouragement? Annoyance? Determination? Fear? Something else?

4. What blessings of perseverance do you hope you will receive, when you choose by faith to persevere?

A Petition to Bring to God

I made reference in *It's Okay Not to Be Okay* that there came a day when I was so frustrated, so fed up with the fight, so ready to be done with the pain that this life seems to take pleasure in doling out, that there on the floor of my psych-hospital room I begged God to take my life. Like the prophet Elijah, I'd had enough. Like Elijah, I was done. Like Elijah, I just wanted to sleep. And perhaps to never, ever wake up.

In that story from 1 Kings, we find this scene:

Now Ahab told Jezebel everything Elijah had done and how he had killed all the prophets with the sword. So Jezebel sent a messenger to Elijah to say, "May the gods deal with me, be it ever so severely, if by this time tomorrow I do not make your life like that of one of them."

Elijah was afraid and ran for his life. When he came to Beersheba in Judah, he left his servant there, while he himself went a day's journey into the wilderness. He came to a broom bush, sat down under it and prayed that he might die. "I have had enough, LORD," he said. "Take my life; I am no better than my ancestors." Then he lay down under the bush and fell asleep.

All at once an angel touched him and said, "Get up and eat." He looked around, and there by his head was some bread baked over hot coals, and a jar of water. He ate and drank and then lay down again.

The angel of the LORD came back a second time and touched him and said, "Get up and eat, for the journey is too much for you." So he got up and ate and drank. Strengthened by that food, he traveled forty days and forty nights until he reached Horeb, the mountain of God. There he went into a cave and spent the night.

And the word of the LORD came to him: "What are you doing here, Elijah?"

He replied, "I have been very zealous for the LORD God Almighty. The Israelites have rejected your covenant, torn down your altars, and put your prophets to death with the sword. I am the only one left, and now they are trying to kill me too."

The LORD said, "Go out and stand on the mountain in the presence of the LORD, for the LORD is about to pass by."

Then a great and powerful wind tore the mountains apart and shattered the rocks before the LORD, but the LORD was not in the wind. After the wind there was an earthquake, but the LORD was not in the earthquake. After the earthquake came a fire, but the LORD was not in the fire. And after the fire came a gentle whisper. When Elijah heard it, he pulled his cloak over his face and went out and stood at the mouth of the cave. (19:1–13)

This account stuns me every time. Far from rebuking his weary servant, God cooks him dinner while the man takes a nap. And then, as if that were not enough, God shows up for Elijah . . . as in, *literally* shows up.

Perhaps you can relate to Elijah—and to me. Perhaps the fight has been too much for you, and you're ready to lie down or give up. Perhaps you're disillusioned by the fact that the control you thought you wielded in your life was an outright sham the entire time.

Whatever your circumstances, and whatever level of distress you find yourself in today, may I invite you to trust God all over again with the circumstances and needs—both the overwhelming and the painfully practical aspects—of your life?

What I've compiled for you below is a list of seven of the names of God and what they tell us about who He is. There are more than these seven, of course. But I wonder if one of these seven speaks powerfully and precisely to your needs right here, right now.

Read the name—aloud, if you prefer. Read the meaning of this glorious name. And then read the verse or the account that follows. Which name resonates most with you, and why? Which aspect of the nature of God do you need to hold on to today?

Elohim: The Strong Creator God

> But to us there is but one God, the Father, of whom are all things, and we in him; and one Lord Jesus Christ, by whom are all things, and we by him. (1 Cor. 8:6 KJV)

Adonai: Lord of All

> And there is salvation in no one else, for there is no other name under heaven given among men by which we must be saved. (Acts 4:12 ESV)

El Roi: The God Who Sees Me

Now Sarai, Abram's wife, had borne him no children. But she had an Egyptian slave named Hagar; so she said to Abram, "The LORD has kept me from having children. Go, sleep with my slave; perhaps I can build a family through her."

Abram agreed to what Sarai said. So after Abram had been living in Canaan ten years, Sarai his wife took her Egyptian slave Hagar and gave her to her husband to be his wife. He slept with Hagar, and she conceived.

When she knew she was pregnant, she began to despise her mistress. Then Sarai said to Abram, "You are responsible for the wrong I am suffering. I put my slave in your arms, and now that she knows she is pregnant, she despises me. May the LORD judge between you and me."

"Your slave is in your hands," Abram said. "Do with her whatever you think best." Then Sarai mistreated Hagar; so she fled from her.

The angel of the LORD found Hagar near a spring in the desert; it was the spring that is beside the road to Shur. And he said, "Hagar, slave of Sarai, where have you come from, and where are you going?"

"I'm running away from my mistress Sarai," she answered.

Then the angel of the LORD told her, "Go back to your mistress and submit to her." The angel added, "I will increase your descendants so much that they will be too numerous to count."

The angel of the LORD also said to her:

"You are now pregnant
    and you will give birth to a son.
You shall name him Ishmael,
    for the LORD has heard of your misery.
He will be a wild donkey of a man;
    his hand will be against everyone
    and everyone's hand against him,
and he will live in hostility
    toward all his brothers."

She gave this name to the LORD who spoke to her: "You are the God who sees me," for she said, "I have now seen the One who sees me." That is why the well was called Beer Lahai Roi; it is still there, between Kadesh and Bered. (Gen. 16:1–14)

El Shaddai: God Almighty

When Abram was ninety-nine years old, the LORD appeared to him and said, "I am God Almighty; walk before me faithfully and be blameless. Then I will make my covenant between me and you and will greatly increase your numbers."

Abram fell facedown, and God said to him, "As for me, this is my covenant with you: You will be the father of many nations. No longer will you be called Abram; your name will be Abraham, for I have made you a father of many nations. I will make you very fruitful; I will make nations of you, and kings will come from you. I will establish my covenant as an everlasting covenant between me and you and your descendants after you for the generations to come, to be your God and the God of your descendants after you. The whole land of Canaan, where you now reside as a foreigner, I will give as an everlasting possession to you and your descendants after you; and I will be their God." (Gen. 17:1–8)

Jehovah-Shalom: The God of Peace

The Israelites did evil in the eyes of the LORD, and for seven years he gave them into the hands of the Midianites. Because the power of Midian was so oppressive, the Israelites prepared shelters for themselves in mountain clefts, caves and strongholds. Whenever the Israelites planted their crops, the Midianites, Amalekites and other eastern peoples invaded the country. They camped on the land and ruined the crops all the way to Gaza and did not spare a living thing for Israel, neither sheep nor cattle nor donkeys. They came up with their livestock and their tents like swarms of locusts. It was impossible to count them or their camels; they invaded the land to ravage it. Midian so impoverished the Israelites that they cried out to the LORD for help.

When the Israelites cried out to the LORD because of Midian, he sent them a prophet, who said, "This is what the LORD, the God of Israel, says: I brought you up out of Egypt, out of the land of slavery. I rescued you from the hand of the Egyptians. And I delivered you from the hand of all your oppressors; I drove them out before you and gave you their land. I said to you, 'I am the LORD your God; do not worship the gods of the Amorites, in whose land you live.' But you have not listened to me."

The angel of the LORD came and sat down under the oak in Ophrah that belonged to Joash the Abiezrite, where his son Gideon was threshing wheat in a winepress to keep it from the Midianites. When the angel of the LORD appeared to Gideon, he said, "The LORD is with you, mighty warrior."

"Pardon me, my lord," Gideon replied, "but if the LORD is with us, why has all this happened to us? Where are all his wonders that our ancestors told us about when they said, 'Did not the LORD bring us up out of Egypt?' But now the LORD has abandoned us and given us into the hand of Midian."

The LORD turned to him and said, "Go in the strength you have and save Israel out of Midian's hand. Am I not sending you?"

"Pardon me, my lord," Gideon replied, "but how can I save Israel? My clan is the weakest in Manasseh, and I am the least in my family."

The LORD answered, "I will be with you, and you will strike down all the Midianites, leaving none alive."

Gideon replied, "If now I have found favor in your eyes, give me a sign that it is really you talking to me. Please do not go away until I come back and bring my offering and set it before you."

And the LORD said, "I will wait until you return."

Gideon went inside, prepared a young goat, and from an ephah of flour he made bread without yeast. Putting the meat in a basket and its broth in a pot, he brought them out and offered them to him under the oak.

The angel of God said to him, "Take the meat and the unleavened bread, place them on this rock, and pour out the broth." And Gideon did so. Then the angel of the LORD touched the meat and the unleavened bread with the tip of the staff that was in his hand. Fire flared from the rock, consuming the meat and the bread. And the angel of the LORD disappeared. When Gideon realized that it was the angel of the LORD, he exclaimed, "Alas, Sovereign LORD! I have seen the angel of the LORD face to face!"

But the LORD said to him, "Peace! Do not be afraid. You are not going to die."

So Gideon built an altar to the LORD there and called it The LORD Is Peace. To this day it stands in Ophrah of the Abiezrites. (Judg. 6:1–24)

Jehovah-Rapha: The God Who Heals

I will exalt you, LORD,
for you lifted me out of the depths
and did not let my enemies gloat over me.
LORD my God, I called to you for help,
and you healed me.
You, LORD, brought me up from the realm of the dead;
you spared me from going down to the pit.
Sing the praises of the LORD, you his faithful people;
praise his holy name.
For his anger lasts only a moment,
but his favor lasts a lifetime;
weeping may stay for the night,
but rejoicing comes in the morning.
When I felt secure, I said,
"I will never be shaken."
LORD, when you favored me,
you made my royal mountain stand firm;
but when you hid your face,
I was dismayed.

To you, LORD, I called;
   to the Lord I cried for mercy:
"What is gained if I am silenced,
   if I go down to the pit?
Will the dust praise you?
   Will it proclaim your faithfulness?
Hear, LORD, and be merciful to me;
   LORD, be my help."
You turned my wailing into dancing;
   you removed my sackcloth and clothed me with joy,
that my heart may sing your praises and not be silent.
   LORD my God, I will praise you forever. (Ps. 30:1–12)

Jehovah-Raah: The Lord Is My Shepherd

The LORD is my shepherd, I lack nothing.
   He makes me lie down in green pastures,
he leads me beside quiet waters,
   he refreshes my soul.
He guides me along the right paths
   for his name's sake.
Even though I walk
   through the darkest valley,
I will fear no evil,
   for you are with me;
your rod and your staff,
   they comfort me.
You prepare a table before me
   in the presence of my enemies.
You anoint my head with oil;
   my cup overflows.
Surely your goodness and love will follow me
   all the days of my life,
and I will dwell in the house of the LORD
   forever. (Ps. 23:1–6)

Below, note the name you selected from the seven names listed above. Then adapt the rest of the prayer as needed, as you invite God's presence and power into your circumstances.

Father God, today in my life, please show up as . . .

_____

_____

_____

_____

I invite You into my current situation, with all its struggles, with all its confusion and pain. Thank you that You delight in the details of my life, and I choose to be comforted today by Your care. You are a good Father. Holy and just. Merciful and wise. All-knowing and all-seeing. I trust that You see my situation now. I give control to You today, Lord, the control that has belonged to You all along. May I find peace and rest and joy in Your sure grip today. In Jesus's name I pray, amen.

Final Thoughts

It occurs to me that the first Bible verse I learned as a small child was Psalm 46:10, which in part says this: "Be still, and know that I am God." I didn't understand Hebrew derivations at the time, but eventually I would learn that the little phrase "be still" in its original language is *raphah*. *Raphah* means to slacken, to abate, to let go, to let down, to let loose. It is, in the best possible sense of the word, to be relaxed. Isn't that rich? When it comes to relinquishing control of our circumstances, our situations, our very lives, God has written us a permission slip to skip class, to not worry, to simply let it go.

I hope you'll take that permission slip and tape it to your heart today. Whenever you're tempted to wrangle control out of God's hands, glance at that slip and remember that He's got everything—including you—under His beautiful, loving control.

Making These Themes Your Own

- Review the meaning of each of the seven names of God.
- In a posture of prayer, tell God how you long for Him to be in your situation today. Trust Him to do that for you.

six

Rise Above Disappointment

Some unexpected changes in life are welcome, but no one imagines the hard things that wait just around the corner. How do we live, then, when we find ourselves in a place that's far from the life we imagined?

—chapter 6, *It's Okay Not to Be Okay*

Of all the emotions a human can experience, disappointment must be one of the hardest. I'm not fond of rage. Or of envy. Or of regret or confusion or fear. But there's a certain weight to disappointment that really sets it apart. The term itself explains this grievous gravity: we establish—*appoint*—a certain hope for some reality that gets literally dissed in the end. All that eager expectation, for nothing. We're up, up, up! And then, to our utter dismay, we're down.

Based on countless conversations with friends, family members, and women I've met at speaking events, I know I'm not alone in my frustration over disappointment, how it steals something precious from our lives. We are faithful to look heavenward and admit our struggle and change our thoughts. We allow the great what-if exchange to have its way—we let go of our need for control. But instead of feeling gratified by these righteous action steps, we are left with empty hands. *So this is how my life is going to be*, we think, with a sinking heart. *This must be all there is.*

What I want to say to you in this session, if you've ever felt emotions such as these surge through you, is that this *isn't* all there is to life. There is richness you haven't yet tapped. There is an appointment that will never fail you. There is an approach that won't let you down.

> **WHAT'S NOT OKAY**
>
> *I'm more devoted, and yet more disappointed, than ever.*
>
> **WHAT'S BEEN OKAY ALL ALONG**
>
> *God's got me right where I need to be.*

One to Ponder

How would you characterize the most significant disappointments you've known over time? Are they relational in nature? Financial? Educational or vocational? Something else entirely?

Turning to Scripture

As we've noted, the book of Romans is considered by most scholars to be the most theologically rich book in the New Testament. It presents, in painstaking clarity, the reason for the gospel, the relevance of the gospel, the challenges of gospel living, and the blessings one can expect for honoring God's will and ways.

Throughout my life, and especially during some of the darkest seasons of despair I've known, I have taken great comfort in a single verse tucked away in chapter 5 of that letter from the apostle Paul to the church in Rome. In the translation I remember, it reads this way: "Hope does not disappoint, because the love of God has been poured out within our hearts through the Holy Spirit who was given to us" (v. 5 NASB).

Hope does not disappoint. It's a marvelous promise, I think.

The question that remains, I suppose, is, Well, then, how do we get more hope?

Before we attempt to answer that question, let's look at the fuller context of Paul's remarks.

> Therefore, since we have been justified through faith, we have peace with God through our Lord Jesus Christ, through whom we have gained access by faith into this grace in which we now stand. And we boast in the hope of the glory of God. Not only so, but we also glory in our sufferings, because we know that suffering produces perseverance; perseverance, character; and character, hope. And hope does not put us to shame, because God's love has been poured out into our hearts through the Holy Spirit, who has been given to us.
>
> You see, at just the right time, when we were still powerless, Christ died for the ungodly. Very rarely will anyone die for a righteous person, though for a good person someone might possibly dare to die. But God demonstrates his own love for us in this: While we were still sinners, Christ died for us.
>
> Since we have now been justified by his blood, how much more shall we be saved from God's wrath through him! For if, while we were God's enemies, we were reconciled to him through the death of his Son, how much more, having been reconciled, shall we be saved through his life! Not only is this so, but we also boast in God through our Lord Jesus Christ, through whom we have now received reconciliation. (vv. 1–11)

Now, it would be easy to skim this passage and completely miss the point. I don't want us to do that. I want to invite you into a more thoughtful understanding of Paul's thoughts than perhaps you've considered before. This passage can single-handedly set us up for long-term success . . . for a life that is quite astoundingly *disappointment-free*.

Questions for Reflection

Regarding the passage . . .

1. In the New International Version translation of this passage, cited above, this idea of hope that does not disappoint is rendered "hope does not put us to shame." What do you see as the connection between these two terms, *shame* and *disappointment*?

_____

_____

_____

2. What does Paul note as the four-step progression that ends in hope?

_____ produces _____, which produces _____, which produces hope.

3. How do you feel about step 1 in this progression? Do you believe you could develop perseverance apart from enduring troubles and tribulation in this life? If so, how?

_____

_____

4. Based on the eventual hope that is born of the Christ-follower's pain, what do you suppose it means to "glory in our sufferings"?

_____

_____

_____

IT'S OKAY NOT TO BE OKAY STUDY GUIDE

Regarding your personal life . . .

1. It seems from this passage that because there is a hope that does not disappoint, there also is a hope that does. In your experience, what types of things have you hoped in or hoped for that could never fulfill you in the end?

2. We see throughout the New Testament an emphasis on joining Christ not only in his redemptive mission throughout the earth but also in his *suffering*. His transformative work in our lives, then, is far more about developing our character than about feeding our comfort. And yet here in Romans 5, we discover that there are seven clear benefits to letting noble character have its way.

In the following list, recast each of the seven benefits in your own words.

- "We have peace with God through our Lord Jesus Christ" (v. 1).

- "We have gained access by faith into this grace in which we now stand" (v. 2).

- "We boast in the hope of the glory of God" (v. 2).

  _____

  _____

- "We also glory in our sufferings," because suffering leads to hope (vv. 3–4).

  _____

  _____

- "Since we have now been justified by his blood, how much more shall we be saved from God's wrath through him" (v. 9).

  _____

  _____

- "We also boast in God through our Lord Jesus Christ" (v. 11).

  _____

  _____

- "We have now received reconciliation" (v. 11).

  _____

  _____

3. Reinforcing the idea that suffering indeed yields hope, the writer of Hebrews says, "No discipline seems pleasant at the time, but painful. Later on, however, it produces a harvest of righteousness and peace for those who have been trained by it" (12:11). Can you relate? In your own life, when have you known

"a harvest of righteousness and peace" as a result of being "trained by" discipline?

_____

_____

A Petition to Bring to God

This is next-level discipleship. Learning to discipline ourselves to see trials not as soul-crushing burdens but as agents of blessing is a sign of spiritual growth. And yet isn't such a posture worth it if it means never being disappointed again?

> **dikaisune**
> *[dik-ah-yos-'oo-nay]*
> Equity, justification, righteousness.

For the next several minutes, take another look at the seven benefits you summarized in your own words above. Which of the seven do you most need to be reminded of today? Select from the list below and then offer a prayer of petition to God, jotting it below if you like, inviting His transformative work in that specific area.

- Peace with God
- Access to grace
- The hope of glory
- Certainty of suffering's endgame
- Deliverance from God's wrath
- Confidence in God
- Reconciliation with God

_____

_____

Final Thoughts

When we are in the thick of pain and struggle, it can feel nearly impossible to consider that something good could come of it, and yet that is precisely what the Word of God promises to those who persevere. If you're like me and need a fairly constant reminder that there is a *hope* that won't disappoint, that there is a *way* that won't let us down, then consider memorizing the seven benefits you learned in this session to carry them with you all of your days.

Making These Themes Your Own

- Review the seven blessings of suffering.
- Look behind your toughest circumstances. What blessings do you find hiding there?

seven

Celebrate Your Scars as Tattoos of Triumph

You and I know that terrible things happen in this world. Children are sexually abused, wives are beaten, men lose their wives to breast cancer or find themselves out of a job at an age when it will be harder to find another. The list is long and hard. When we come to faith in Christ, we are offered healing and hope. This is never a quick fix. It can take years to begin to walk away from the things that wounded us so deeply, but as we continue to walk with Christ, His presence becomes greater than the wound, and a scar forms. Our scars are proof that God heals.

—chapter 7, *It's Okay Not to Be Okay*

It has been said that one of the most powerful phrases in the English language is the two-word phrase "Me too." I write this guide in a day when the phrase "Me too" is tightly associated with protests—on social media platforms, primarily—against the sexual harassment of women. Indeed, it is important for sufferers of abuse of any kind to feel safe divulging the abuse. It is therefore no small thing for those sufferers to know that there are countless others who have been willing to say, "You have experienced this devastating pain? Me too. You're not alone." And yet you and I both know that there are countless arenas where we long to find understanding and genuine empathy. To experience *any* unwelcomed shift in life—fear over a newborn's sickness, distress over the loss of a friendship, sudden and out-of-control emotions—is to long for compassionate understanding

> **WHAT'S NOT OKAY**
>
> *The remnants of my suffering are with me still.*
>
> **WHAT'S BEEN OKAY ALL ALONG**
>
> *My "scars" can help others and bring glory to God.*

from someone, somewhere. We long to hear those words that shatter the perceived isolation: "Me too."

One to Ponder

Describe a time when you've been relieved—or perhaps even rescued—by the sound of another's "Me too." What were the circumstances involved? Why were those words so powerful for you to hear?

Turning to Scripture

Following Jesus's resurrection, his disciples didn't quite know what to believe. Their Master, their Teacher, their Rabbi had been taken from them in a most brutal manner; what were they supposed to do now?

Upon seeing Jesus appear before them, they hesitated to rejoice. Was it really *Him*? Had Jesus really been raised from the *dead*? In John 20, we find this scene:

> On the evening of that first day of the week [following Jesus's resurrection], when the disciples were together, with the doors locked for fear of the Jewish leaders, Jesus came and stood among them and

75

said, "Peace be with you!" After he said this, he showed them his hands and side. The disciples were overjoyed when they saw the Lord.

Again Jesus said, "Peace be with you! As the Father has sent me, I am sending you." And with that he breathed on them and said, "Receive the Holy Spirit. If you forgive anyone's sins, their sins are forgiven; if you do not forgive them, they are not forgiven."

Now Thomas (also known as Didymus), one of the Twelve, was not with the disciples when Jesus came. So the other disciples told him, "We have seen the Lord!"

But he said to them, "Unless I see the nail marks in his hands and put my finger where the nails were, and put my hand into his side, I will not believe."

A week later his disciples were in the house again, and Thomas was with them. Though the doors were locked, Jesus came and stood among them and said, "Peace be with you!" Then he said to Thomas, "Put your finger here; see my hands. Reach out your hand and put it into my side. Stop doubting and believe."

Thomas said to him, "My Lord and my God!"

Then Jesus told him, "Because you have seen me, you have believed; blessed are those who have not seen and yet have believed."

Jesus performed many other signs in the presence of his disciples, which are not recorded in this book. But these are written that you may believe that Jesus is the Messiah, the Son of God, and that by believing you may have life in his name. (vv. 19–31)

It really was the Messiah, incarnate, once dead but now fully alive. The wounded Healer had returned to those He'd once healed, His suffering, His scars, still at hand.

Questions for Reflection

Regarding the passage . . .

1. It is commonly thought that because Jesus evidently walked right through a locked door to get to His disciples, His comment "Peace be with you" was an encouragement for them not to freak out, believing they'd seen a ghost. But why else do you suppose Jesus chose that phrase, "Peace be with you," as His first postresurrection words to those who had loved Him most?

2. Just after speaking peace over His friends and disciples, Jesus showed them His pierced hands and side. What was Jesus's purpose in showing them His hard-won scars?

3. What emotion do you suspect motivated Thomas's declaration that unless he saw and felt Jesus's scars for himself, he would not believe it was Christ? The fear of being disappointed? Skepticism? Distrust? Something else?

Regarding your personal life . . .

1. How likely would you have been to insist, as Thomas did, on seeing Jesus's scars before you believed it truly was Him? What

attitudes, assumptions, mistrust, or experiences factor into your perspective here?

_____

_____

2. Based on the plentiful miracles Jesus performed during His earthly ministry, it is reasonable to assume that He could have healed His hands and His side, removing any signs of the pain He had endured. Why do you suppose He kept His scars intact prior to appearing to those He had led?

_____

_____

3. When Thomas said he wanted to see the "nail marks" (v. 25), he used the word *tupos*, which is a noun form of the verb *tupto*. To "tupto" was to pummel, strike, smite, beat, or bash by repeated blows for the purpose of punishment. What thoughts do you imagine went through Jesus's mind as He held out His hands to Thomas and as He pulled up His tunic to reveal His side?

> **tupto** *['toop-to]*
> To cudgel or pummel by repeated blows; to punish, to beat, smite, strike, wound.

_____

_____

What might Thomas have thought?

_____

_____

4. If you were to allow another person to place a finger on your most striking "scars," what scars would you point them to? What suffering led to them, and what "shadow pains" exist still today? On the grid below, note the scars that come to mind as well as any other pertinent information regarding the pain you endured that led to them and the pain you continue to experience even now.

The Scar	The Suffering	Residual Effects

A Petition to Bring to God

I wrote that "our scars are proof that God heals," and while I believe those words are self-explanatory, they carry an important implication I would hate for us to miss. It is true that the scars we bear and wear each day of our lives prove to our own failing hearts that we've been healed. The battle that threatened to take us out of the game did not get its way in the end. Hallelujah! What a profound victory that is.

But if we were to tuck away this information in the folds of our hearts, failing to make it known, what a loss that would be for the kingdom! What a grand opportunity we'd miss. In the same way that Jesus *willingly*, *enthusiastically*, and *patiently* invited His disciples to scrutinize His scars so that His Father would receive glory and so that God's fame in the earth would increase, we too can invite others to see where we've suffered for the purpose of glorifying God.

"Yes, my suffering was real," we might say. "And yes, I believed all hope was lost. But look! I've got proof! I made it out! I survived, and so can you."

For many years, I wrestled with whether to share with the world my story of mental illness, emotional pain, and chronic suicidal thoughts. I worried over being misunderstood. I worried about putting those thoughts into someone else's mind. I worried over how my family would feel about my sharing such intimate details of my life. But then I sat with this scene involving Jesus and His disciples, and I thought, *Our scars too bear testimony to God's miraculous healing power.*

To refuse to show those we're ministering to how we've suffered and how through Christ we've prevailed is to set them up for a lifetime of pain and disillusionment as they feel abandoned to life's punishing surprises.

But there's more. What I discovered upon sharing my scars was that I became more and more healed. As I whispered "Me too" and revealed my nail prints, I heard "Me too" in return. It's as though merely mentioning my suffering defanged it somehow; it held far less sway over me. Jesus modeled something important for us: by showing where we've been and telling how we made it out alive, we spread to others who are hopeless the good news that hope lives on.

If you've never done so before, I invite you to work through some of your own scars, asking God to show you how they might serve someone else well. Bring Him the pain you've endured and the process of healing you still find yourself walking through. But don't stop there. Ask Him the following questions, and then wait patiently for His reply.

The scar I bear:

The healing process I'm still walking through:

My petitions, my requests, of God:

Father, who might benefit from knowing of this particular struggle, and how should I share my story with them?

God, which aspects of my suffering are appropriate to mention, and which are best left unspoken for now?

What good might You weave together as I'm faithful to bring glory to You?

Impressions and promptings from God:

_____

_____

_____

The scar I bear:

_____

_____

_____

The healing process I'm still walking through:

_____

_____

_____

My petitions, my requests, of God:

Father, who might benefit from knowing of this particular struggle, and how should I share my story with them?

God, which aspects of my suffering are appropriate to mention, and which are best left unspoken for now?

What good might You weave together as I'm faithful to bring glory to You?

Impressions and promptings from God:

_____

_____

_____

The scar I bear: ✦

_____

_____

_____

The healing process I'm still walking through:

_____

_____

_____

My petitions, my requests, of God:

Father, who might benefit from knowing of this particular struggle, and how should I share my story with them?

God, which aspects of my suffering are appropriate to mention, and which are best left unspoken for now?

What good might You weave together as I'm faithful to bring glory to You?

Impressions and promptings from God:

_____

_____

_____

Final Thoughts

What thoughts or feelings, or fears or insecurities, or hopes or expectations are stirred up in you as you consider that your pain could be used by God for a specific and hope-filled purpose in someone else's life? Spend a few moments logging your thoughts before leaving this session.

_____

_____

_____

Making These Themes Your Own

- Take another look at the scars you bear. Thank God for their presence.
- Ask God who might benefit from knowing the story of the blow that left a particular scar. Who might take encouragement from the fact that you prevailed?
- Be willing to share your story with another. Boldly go where God asks you to go.

eight

Decide to Start Again
... and Again

Don't miss the simple steps. Don't think that they don't matter. For me, taking one step at a time has become a daily act of worship. It's aligning my heart and mind with who God says I am. I would love to say that at this stage in my life I have arrived, but I am still very much on this journey with you.

—chapter 8, *It's Okay Not to Be Okay*

One of the most common themes I hear, whenever I talk to people following one of my messages, is this one: "Sheila, I have been suffering for so long. When will things get better? When will I feel better? When will I *be* better?"

Questions along these lines always take me back to the psalmist's words in Psalm 40: "I waited patiently for the LORD; he turned to me and heard my cry. He lifted me out of the slimy pit, out of the mud and mire; he set my feet on a rock and gave me a firm place to stand. He put a new song in my mouth, a hymn of praise to our God" (vv. 1–3). In the early 1980s, the band U2 recorded a song titled

> **WHAT'S NOT OKAY**
>
> *Despite all my efforts and all this time, I'm clearly not "there" yet.*
>
> **WHAT'S BEEN OKAY ALL ALONG**
>
> *I am who God says I am, and God is doing what he said he would do.*

"40" that centered on this psalm and included in the chorus, "I will sing, sing a new song. . . . How long to sing this song?"

We can relate to these lyrics, can't we? Yes, we believe that the time will come when at last we will sing a new song. But how long will we be made to wait before that longed-for day finally dawns?

One to Ponder

When have you experienced what felt like an interminable delay? What were you waiting for, and what circumstances collided to interfere with getting it?

Turning to Scripture

In the following passage from 2 Corinthians, Paul offers compelling evidence that regardless of how stuck we feel from time to time, the fresh start, the new beginning, the clean slate we seek is already ours.

> If we are "out of our mind," as some say, it is for God; if we are in our right mind, it is for you. For Christ's love compels us, because we are convinced that one died for all, and therefore all died. And he died for all, that those who live should no longer live for themselves but for him who died for them and was raised again.
>
> So from now on we regard no one from a worldly point of view. Though we once regarded Christ in this way, we do so no longer. Therefore, if anyone is in Christ, the new creation has come: The old has gone, the new is here! All this is from God, who reconciled us to himself through Christ and gave us the ministry of reconciliation: that God was reconciling the world to himself in Christ, not counting people's sins against them. And he has committed to us the message of reconciliation. We are therefore Christ's ambassadors, as

though God were making his appeal through us. We implore you on Christ's behalf: Be reconciled to God. God made him who had no sin to be sin for us, so that in him we might become the righteousness of God. (5:13–21)

For those of us in Christ, these verses promise that something profoundly new has come. New ... fresh ... *kainos*, in the Greek. Long-awaited new life that actually sticks around.

> **kainos** *[kahee-'nos]*
> New, fresh.

The old is gone.

The new has come.

Who doesn't want in on *that*?

Questions for Reflection

Regarding the passage . . .

In the Amplified Bible, 2 Corinthians 5:17 reads this way:

> Therefore if anyone is in Christ [that is, grafted in, joined to Him by faith in Him as Savior], he is a new creature [reborn and renewed by the Holy Spirit]; the old things [the previous moral and spiritual condition] have passed away. Behold, new things have come [because spiritual awakening brings a new life].

Given this additional insight, how would you describe in your own words what each of the following concepts means?

Being "in Christ"

_____

_____

_____

87

The "old things" that have passed away

_____

_____

The "new things" that have come

_____

_____

Regarding your personal life . . .

1. Based on your firsthand experience, is this a one-time affair of ushering out the old and ushering in the new, or is it an experience that must happen time and again?

_____

_____

2. What action step do the last few lines of the passage encourage as a means for dealing with the temporary gap that exists between Christ's perfect reflection of the new we long for and our imperfect manifestation of that state?

_____

_____

3. What might it mean for you to be "reconciled to God" from the depths of your darkness and despair?

_____

_____

4. What other attitudes, assumptions, and actions do you suppose would naturally fall away if you were to focus your attention not on your troubling circumstances but on being reconciled—here, now, in this moment—to your heavenly Father instead? How might such an effort help reveal the "new" that Christ died to usher in?

A Petition to Bring to God

A profound realization I've made is that sometimes the "new" that God is bringing about happens not externally, in my circumstances, but internally, in my own mind and heart. I'm not alone, it turns out. The more people I talk with, the more I see this inside-job dynamic occurring, where the new thing brought about is a simple perspective shift, a change of mind.

In *It's Okay Not to Be Okay*, I wrote about a man I met following a speaking engagement who stunned me with his outlook and peace. He approached me after having waited a full hour as I signed copies of my latest book for others. As he stood there patiently, I couldn't help but notice the striking young woman at his side—his daughter, I'd later learn. He introduced himself and then told me what he'd been waiting there to say. Here's what I wrote:

> He touched the right side of his face, which was badly scarred, and told me in a faint, scratchy voice that when he was fifteen he had tried to kill himself. He put a loaded gun under his chin and fired. He said that in the millisecond between pulling the trigger and the bullet entering his skull he heard Christ ask him if he wanted to live. He said yes.

He was now in his forties with six children, one of them the beautiful young girl who was by his side. I was overwhelmed by his story. . . . He told me that the bullet is still in his skull, as it would be too dangerous to remove, and that his voice is permanently damaged. I asked him if that was a harsh reminder of his pain. He told me that it was the absolute opposite. He said that he has a daily reminder of the grace and mercy of God. He has learned to love the brokenness in himself and offer it to Christ. He plans to start an outreach to young people who might be in the same place he was when he was fifteen years old.

The truth about our lives is that we are all broken. It's more obvious when the scar is on the skin and not on the soul, but we are broken nonetheless. The decision we get to make is whether we hide that brokenness or offer it to Jesus.[1]

What thoughts or emotions come to mind as you take in this man's story? What is your reaction to it?

_____

_____

_____

How do you think you would have responded to life had you been that fifteen-year-old trying to move on?

_____

_____

_____

For this man, the physical evidence of his brokenness—in this case, a bullet fired from his own gun—reminded him of "the grace and mercy of God." What a massive shift in perspective from the one I'd proposed, that of seeing it as something harsh. Below, describe the attitude you believe a person must possess to see *blessing* where others see burden, to glean *spiritual fruit* from undeniable pain.

If you'd like to invite a similar perspective shift regarding the burden you presently bear, work through the following guided prompts, asking God to (literally) change your mind.

Father, I'm weary from this present pain, from these circumstances too heavy to bear. I speak them aloud to You now.

I long for the newness Paul spoke about, for the freshness, the novelty, the spark. If I were to put this longing into my own words, I'd tell You that . . .

God, I wonder if the newness You're ushering in is about my situation or about me. My thoughts on this issue, if I'm being candid, are . . .

My hope is that You'll give me new thoughts to think, a new perspective to consider, a brand-new song to sing. The lyrics of that song, I pray, will sound like this:

Final Thoughts

Sometimes I wonder if the reason we have trouble embracing the new that God longs to usher into our lives is that we are clinging so tightly to the old. May we loosen our grip today.

You can do this! Simply begin to open your hand.

Making These Themes Your Own

- Ask God what new He is ushering into your life—a new set of circumstances, a new relationship, a new perspective, a new thought to think, something else.
- Hold fast to that new thing today, choosing to believe it will bring hope to your heart.

A Word of Thanks

Well done! You made it to the end of this leg of the journey, and I can't tell you how happy I am that you made it with me. I know that some of the steps we took were far easier than others, but look . . . we persevered. And the blessings of perseverance are reserved for those who do just that.

What are those blessings? An increasing sense of fearlessness, for one. Confidence in Christ. Deep-seated joy. The genuine belief that regardless of what we've been through, we will make it through alive. I could go on here, but I think you catch my point: as we continue to walk toward Jesus, our circumstances stop walking all over us. Yes, tough times will still show up, but they no longer have to take us down.

As I was putting the finishing touches on this guide, a series of unforeseen publishing hiccups nearly kept it from seeing the light of day. There was a time when that reality would have sent me tumbling toward despair. But do you know what arrested that fall? It was the still, small whisper of Jesus, reminding me for the millionth time, *I've got this.*

He *does* have this.

He has it *all.*

He has you and me. He has us both in His safe, strong grip.

My hope is that from this day forward, whenever you're tempted to take a tumble, you'll remember that simple truth.

Jesus has this.

Jesus has me.

All will be okay.

Notes

Session 1

1. All derivations are from James Strong, *Strong's Expanded Exhaustive Concordance of the Bible* (Nashville: Thomas Nelson, 2009).

Session 3

1. Isaac Watts, "When I Survey the Wondrous Cross," 1707, public domain, https://library.timelesstruths.org/music/When_I_Survey_the_Wondrous_Cross/.
2. Sheila Walsh, *It's Okay Not to Be Okay: Moving Forward One Day at a Time* (Grand Rapids: Baker Books, 2018), 66.

Session 8

1. Walsh, *It's Okay Not to Be Okay*, 173–74.